CONTENTS

Some words are shown in bold, **like this**. You can find out what they mean by looking in the glossary.

COULD A ROBOT MAKE MY DINNER?

Robots are already used to make food in factories. So if you have eaten a ready meal, then some sort of robot probably *did* make your dinner!

Scientists have also built robot chefs like the one in the photo, but these are rare and expensive. Who knows, one day, maybe everyone will have one!

This robot chef makes sushi with a hand that looks human!

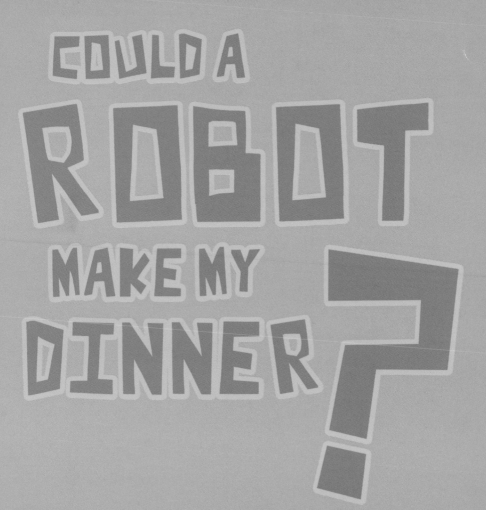

COULD A ROBOT MAKE MY DINNER?

And Other Questions About Technology

Kay Barnham

Raintree

Raintree is an imprint of Capstone Global Library Limited, a company incorporated in England and Wales having its registered office at 7 Pilgrim Street, London, EC4V 6LB – Registered company number: 6695582

www.raintreepublishers.co.uk
myorders@raintreepublishers.co.uk

Text © Capstone Global Library Limited 2014
First published in hardback in 2014
Paperback edition first published in 2015
The moral rights of the proprietor have been asserted.

Edited by Dan Nunn, Rebecca Rissman, and John-Paul Wilkins
Designed by Steve Mead
Picture research by Mica Brancic
Production by Sophia Argyris
Originated by Capstone Global Library Ltd
Printed and bound in China by CTPS

ISBN 978 1 406 25949 0 (hardback)
17 16 15 14 13
10 9 8 7 6 5 4 3 2 1

ISBN 978 1 406 25955 1 (paperback)
18 17 16 15 14
10 9 8 7 6 5 4 3 2 1

British Library Cataloguing in Publication Data
Barnham, Kay.
Could a robot make my dinner? and other questions about technology. -- (Questions you never thought you'd ask)
602-dc23
A full catalogue record for this book is available from the British Library.

Acknowledgements
We would like to thank the following for permission to reproduce photographs: © Frank Pattyn, Laboratoire de Glaciologie, Université Libre de Bruxelles p. 27; Alamy pp. 15 (© Dmitry Mikhaevich), 20 (© PBWPIX), 21 (© Image Source), 29 (© Simon Belcher); Corbis p. 11 (Godong/© Philippe Lissac), 23 (© Roger Ressmeyer), 28 (epa/© Adrian Bradshaw); Getty Images pp. 17 (Gary Williams), 19 (Photolibrary/Rune Johansen); NASA p. 7; Rex Features p. 4 (Sinopix); Shutterstock pp. 5 (© Leonid Shcheglov), 6 (© Hunor Focze), 8 laptop (© iQoncept), 8 bedding (© karam Miri), 9 (© Dmitriy Shironosov), 10 living room (© art&design), 10 magician (© Elnur), 12 painter (© auremar), 12 toothbrush (© Ioannis Pantzi), 13 (© Leah-Anne Thompson), 14 cartoon weight (© Robert Spriggs), 14 crane (© Tonis Pan), 16 computer (© Fer Gregory), 16 goggles (© Rtimages), 16 aeroplane (© PJF), 18 tyrannosaurus (© DM7), 18 person in chemical protection suit (© 3355m), 18 spacecraft (© Jan Kaliciak), 22 futuristic space station (© Andreas Meyer), 22 astronaut (© siraphat), 22 nappy (© Ogonkova), 24 pirate (© Jeanne McRight), 24 house in water (© Lightspring), 25 (© nevenm), 26 snow-capped peaks (© Vadim Petrakov), 26 man holding measuring tape (© luiggi33).

Cover photographs of robot chef (© Julien Tromeur), cheeseburger (© Valentyn Volkov), and chips (© Aaron Amat) reproduced with permission of Shutterstock.

We would like to thank Diana Bentley and Marla Conn for their invaluable help in the preparation of this book.

Every effort has been made to contact copyright holders of any material reproduced in this book. Any omissions will be rectified in subsequent printings if notice is given to the publisher.

Disclaimer

These robots are
making delicious
ice creams!

WHY DO WE NEED ROCKETS TO GET INTO SPACE?

We need rockets to escape the pull of Earth's **gravity**. When a rocket is launched, powerful engines burn rocket fuel. Nozzles point **gases** and flames from the engines downwards. This gives enough **thrust** to speed the rocket upwards and into space.

You couldn't fly to space in a helicopter!

CAN A COMPUTER REALLY CATCH A VIRUS?

Absolutely! But a computer virus is not a disease. It is actually a computer program that spreads from one computer to another, often by email. Just as human viruses can make us poorly, computer viruses can harm computers. Some viruses stop computers working properly. Others delete information stored on them.

Did you know?
A computer virus leaves a copy of itself on each computer it affects.

DO REMOTE CONTROLS WORK BY MAGIC?

Sadly not! Remote controls work by sending out beams of **infrared** light. They can be used to operate TVs, sound systems, and many other devices. Different buttons send different signals, for example to change the channel or turn up the volume. But we can't see infrared light, so the beams are invisible to us!

Did you know?
Some games consoles use infrared light in their wireless controllers.

HOW DO THE STRIPES GET INTO TOOTHPASTE?

To make striped toothpaste, tubes are filled with big stripes of different coloured toothpaste. Then the end of the tube is sealed to keep it inside. When the tube is squeezed, small amounts of each colour are pushed out of the nozzle. These appear as long, much thinner stripes.

Toothpaste is very slippery. When the tube is squeezed, the colours slide past each other and don't get mixed up.

WHY DON'T CRANES FALL OVER?

It's all about balance. To stop it falling over, a crane needs to create enough force to balance the load it is picking up.

Tower cranes have a short arm that carries a weight, and a long arm with a hook for picking things up. As long as the weight and the load are balanced, the crane won't fall over.

VERY HEAVY

WHO FLIES A PILOTLESS AEROPLANE?

Unmanned aerial vehicles – or UAVs – have computers on board so they can fly themselves. They can also be flown by human pilots. But these pilots are down on the ground, not up in the air. UAVs are sent to places where it would be too risky for humans to go.

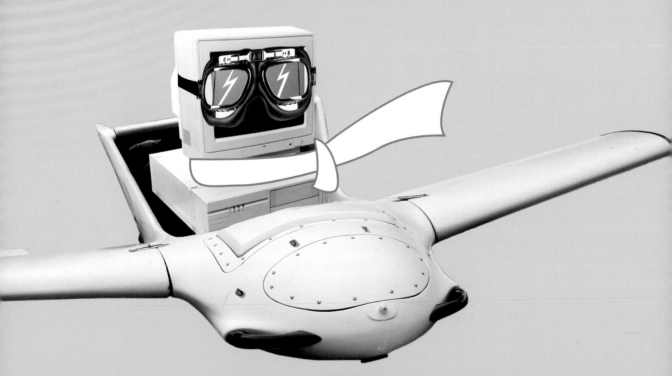

It looks as if these pilots are playing computer games, but they are actually flying real aircraft.

IS TIME TRAVEL POSSIBLE?

Yes. But don't get *too* excited. The closer you get to the speed of light, the slower time gets. So if you were able to travel at millions of kilometres per hour, your watch would go a tiny bit slower and you would travel a little way into the future. But going back in time is impossible.

It's much easier to watch time travel in a sci-fi film than it is to do it in real life.

Did you know?
Scientists at the CERN laboratory have managed to make **particles** travel at speeds close to the speed of light. It would be much more difficult to make people travel that quickly!

WHY DO I NEED SPECIAL GLASSES TO WATCH 3D FILMS?

A **3D** film is not one film, but two! Each one is slightly different. 3D glasses have two different **lenses** so you see one film through one lens and the other film through the other lens. Your brain puts the two images together to make a film look like real 3D.

Did you know?
3D glasses make objects in 3D films appear nearer or further away, just like our eyes see objects (or 'judge distance') in real life!

HOW DO ASTRONAUTS GO TO THE TOILET IN SPACE?

There's no **gravity** in space, which means that everything floats. So if astronauts used a normal toilet, things could get *very* messy! Instead, astronauts use a special toilet or a pipe that uses air rather than water to flush waste away.

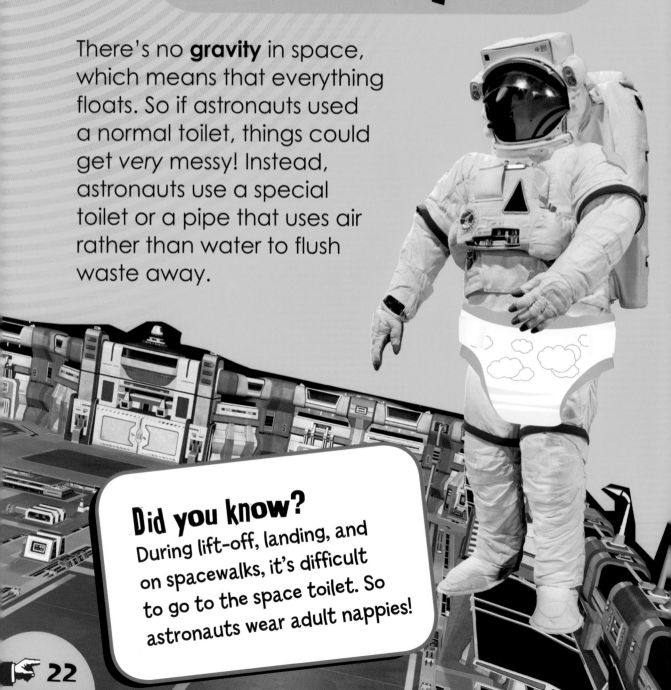

Did you know?
During lift-off, landing, and on spacewalks, it's difficult to go to the space toilet. So astronauts wear adult nappies!

WHY DON'T BOATS SINK?

It's all to do with the weight of a boat and the amount of water it **displaces**.

A boat weighing 100 tonnes sinks into the water until it has displaced 100 tonnes of water. Then, if there is still some of the boat above the water, it floats!

Oh no!

Houses don't float so well!

Some of a boat's **hull** is under the water, out of sight.

HOW DO I MEASURE A MOUNTAIN?

Can you imagine trying to measure a mountain with a ruler? It wouldn't be easy! Instead, you can measure **angles** between the ground and the mountain top. Then you can use a special sum to work out the height. Nowadays, scientists also use measurements from **satellites**, which are even easier and more accurate!

Theodolite

The angle between the ground and a mountain top can be measured with a device called a theodolite.

WHY DO NIGHT-VISION GOGGLES MAKE EVERYTHING GREEN?

Night-vision goggles make even the smallest amount of light thousands of times brighter. First, the eyepiece makes the image bigger. Then it is shone onto a screen coated with a glow-in-the-dark substance called phosphor. This is what makes everything look green!

Did you know?
Green phosphor is used because our eyes can see more shades of green than other phosphor colours.

GLOSSARY

3D something that has three dimensions – height, width, and depth – like objects do in real life

angle size of the corner where two lines meet

displace push out of the way; move elsewhere

gas substance like air that can move about freely

gravity force that pulls everything towards Earth

hull outer shell of a boat

infrared type of light wave not visible to the human eye

lens curved piece of glass or plastic that light can pass through

liquid something runny, like water

particle very, very tiny thing

satellite object that travels around Earth and collects information

solid hard or firm

thrust push

FIND OUT MORE

Books

First Encyclopedia of Science (Usborne, 2011)

Science Experiments, Robert Winston (Dorling Kindersley, 2011)

Space (Up Close), Paul Harrison (Franklin Watts, 2010)

Websites

www.kidsastronomy.com
Discover all there is to know about the solar system and space exploration on this website.

www.sciencemuseum.org.uk
Find out about science on the Science Museum's website. You could even visit the museum to learn more.

INDEX